D1537956

JUN - - 2015

CB

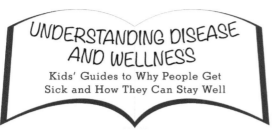

UNDERSTANDING DISEASE
AND WELLNESS
Kids' Guides to Why People Get
Sick and How They Can Stay Well

A KID'S GUIDE TO
ASTHMA

Rae Simons

VILLAGE EARTH PRESS

Series List

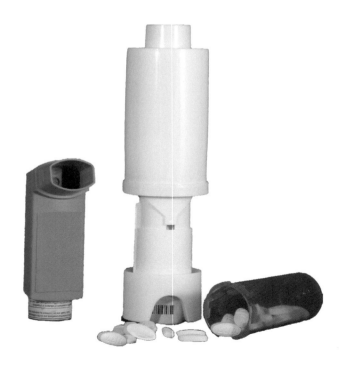

UNDERSTANDING DISEASE
AND WELLNESS
Kids' Guides to Why People Get
Sick and How They Can Stay Well

A KID'S GUIDE TO
ASTHMA

Rae Simons

Understanding Disease and Wellness:
Kids' Guides to Why People Get Sick and How They Can Stay Well
A KID'S GUIDE TO ASTHMA

Village Earth Press
Vestal, New York 13850
www.villageearthpress.com

First Printing
9 8 7 6 5 4 3 2 1

Series ISBN: 978-1-62524-022-4
ISBN: 978-1-62524-035-4
ebook ISBN: 978-1-62524-057-6

Library of Congress Control Number: 2013911250

Author: Simons, Rae

Note: This book is a revised and updated edition of *Why Can't I Breathe? Kids & Asthma* (ISBN: 978-1-934970-15-7), published in 2009 by Alpha House Publishing.

Introduction

According to a recent study reported in the Virginia Henderson International Nursing Library, kids worry about getting sick. They worry about AIDS and cancer, about allergies and the "super-germs" that resist medication. They know about these ills—but they don't always understand what causes them or how they can be prevented.

Unfortunately, most 9- to 11-year-olds, the study found, get their information about diseases like AIDS from friends and television; only 20 percent of the children interviewed based their understanding of illness on facts they had learned at school. Too often, kids believe urban legends, schoolyard folktales, and exaggerated movie plots. Oftentimes, misinformation like this only makes their worries worse. The January 2008 *Child Health News* reported that 55 percent of all children between 9 and 13 "worry almost all the time" about illness.

This series, **Understanding Disease and Wellness**, offers readers clear information on various illnesses and conditions, as well as the immunizations that can prevent many diseases. The books dispel the myths with clearly presented facts and colorful, accurate illustrations. Better yet, these books will help kids understand not only illness—but also what they can do to stay as healthy as possible.

—Dr. Elise Berlan

Just the Facts

- Asthma is a disease that makes the airways to your lungs narrow, making it difficult to breathe.

- Asthma can be passed on to you from your parents, or something around you can trigger it.

- Inhalers, nebulizers, and steroids are all used to treat asthma attacks. Other medicines can keep asthma attacks from happening in the first place.

- Playing wind instruments and sports can actually make your lungs stronger if you have asthma.

- People get asthma all around the world. No cures have been found, but medicines and treatments can help people live with asthma.

What Is Asthma?

Asthma is a *chronic* disease that changes your airways. Your airways are the tubes that carry air in from your mouth and nose to your lungs and then out again. If you have asthma, the inside walls of your airways are inflamed (swollen). This makes the airways very sensitive. They tend to react strongly to anything that irritates them or that triggers an allergic reaction. When the airways react, they get narrower. This means less air can flow through to your lungs. You may start to wheeze. (Wheezing is a whistling sound when you breathe.) It can also make you cough. It can make your chest feel tight. You may have breathing trouble, especially at night and in the early morning.

Words to Know

Chronic: having to do with something that's long-lasting and ongoing (usually a disease).

Your Respiratory System

All the cells in your body need oxygen. Without it, they couldn't move or grow. They couldn't turn food into energy. Without oxygen, you and your cells would die.

Oxygen comes from the air you *inhale* through your nose and mouth. The air flows down through your windpipe. The windpipe divides into two tubes that lead into the lungs.

If you could see your lungs, you might think they looked like big, red sponges. Inside the spongy tissue, tubes called bronchi branch into even smaller tubes. They look like the branches of a tree.

Did You Know?

If you could spread out flat all the air sacs in an adult's lungs, they would cover an area about a third the size of a tennis court!

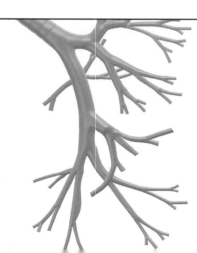

At the end of these tubes are millions of tiny bubbles. These little air sacs are called alveoli. Inside the air sacs, the oxygen from the air you've breathed passes into tiny blood vessels. Then the oxygen is carried in your blood to all your body's cells. The alveoli trade the oxygen for waste products, like carbon dioxide. The carbon dioxide goes back up through your lungs. Then you *exhale* it out through your nose or mouth.

Words to Know

Inhale: breathe in.

Exhale: breathe out.

Asthma Symptoms

The poster on the next page describes how a child with asthma feels. Asthma makes your chest hurt. It makes you gasp for breath. It keeps your respiratory system from working the way it should. It can be a scary feeling.

"WHEN I HAVE AN ASTHMA ATTACK I FEEL LIKE A FISH WITH NO WATER."

–JESSE, AGE 5

ATTACK ASTHMA. ACT NOW.
1-866-NO-ATTACKS
W W W . N O A T T A C K S . O R G

Ad Council | ♲EPA

CDDIS 10/01

13

What Does Asthma Do Inside Your Body?

The reason why asthma makes a person gasp for breath is because of what it does to the inside of the lungs.

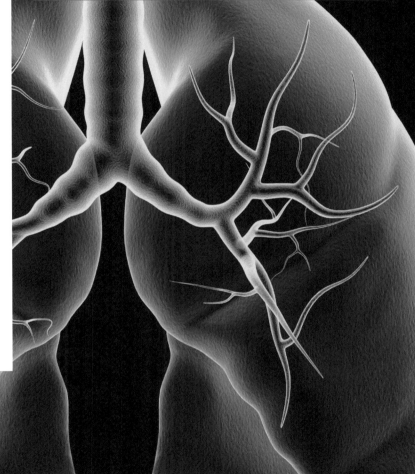

During an asthma attack, the sides of the airways in your lungs swell. This makes the inside of the airways shrink. Less air gets in and out of your lungs. *Mucus* clogs up the airways even more.

ASK THE DOCTOR

Someone told me that if I have asthma, I won't grow as tall. Is that true?

A: No, not if your asthma is being treated by a doctor. Sometimes severe asthma can slow the onset of puberty (the stage where your body starts turning into an adult). This can mean you may get your height later than other kids your age. But so long as you do what your doctor tells you, and your asthma is under good control, your asthma won't get in the way of your growth.

Words to Know

Mucus: a thick, slippery fluid that's made by the linings of your nose, lungs, and throat.

Who Gets Asthma?

Asthma often starts in early childhood. Even babies can have asthma. It is the most common chronic disease in children. Some children outgrow asthma as they get older.

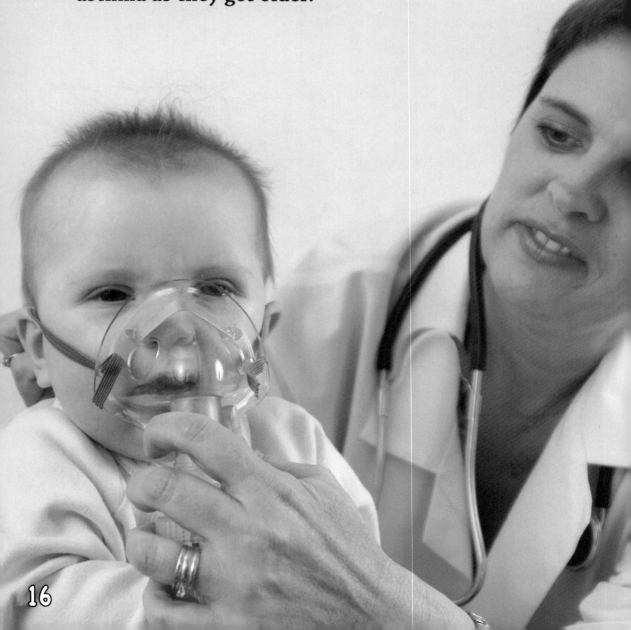

But adults get asthma, too. Around the world, about 300 million people have asthma. People get asthma in every country in the world, but it is more dangerous to people living in *poverty*. More people die from asthma in low-income countries.

Words to Know

Poverty: the condition of being poor (lacking money and/or the basic necessities of life).

What Causes Asthma?

Words to Know

Factors: things that help produce a result.

Pathology of Asthma

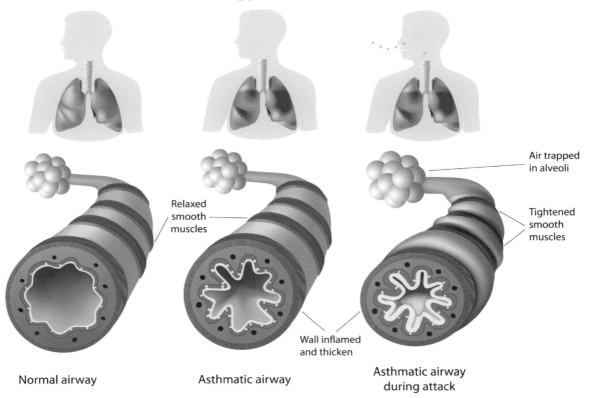

Relaxed smooth muscles

Air trapped in alveoli

Tightened smooth muscles

Wall inflamed and thicken

Normal airway

Asthmatic airway

Asthmatic airway during attack

Asthma is becoming more and more common. In 2009, one in ten children had asthma. There are 25 million people that have asthma, a number that has increased by 4.3 million since 2001. Doctors believe this is because of a number of *factors*. Allergies, poor indoor air quality, and pollution may all play a part.

Allergies

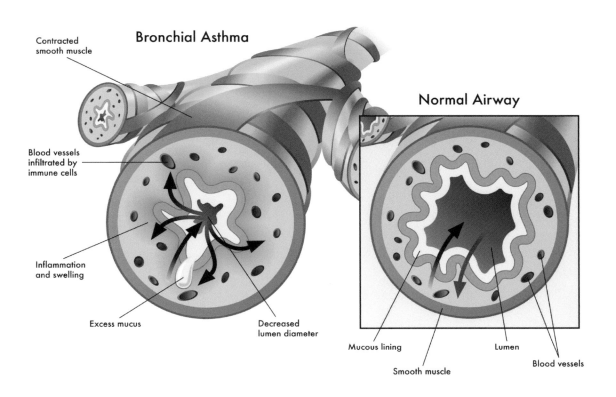

Bronchial Asthma

Contracted
smooth muscle

Blood vessels
infiltrated by
immune cells

Inflammation
and swelling

Excess mucus

Decreased
lumen diameter

Normal Airway

Mucous lining

Lumen

Smooth muscle

Blood vessels

When you're allergic, your body's immune system responds to some harmless material (such as pollen from a flower) as though it were an invading germ. The result is *inflammation* and mucus production. This can trigger asthma in some people.

Words to Know

Inflammation: a condition where your body's tissues become hot, red, and swollen.

Pollution

Pollution is what happens when we make our world dirty. Air pollution (like what's shown here) is made up of chemicals, smoke, and tiny specks of dirt.

Air pollution is one of the things that can trigger asthma. Scientists have shown that air pollution from cars, factories, and power plants is a major cause of asthma attacks. Even people who don't normally have asthma can have a first attack when they breathe air that has a heavy *concentration* of pollution.

Words to Know

Concentration: the amount of some substance per unit of another substance (such as grams per liter).

Secondhand Smoke

Secondhand smoke is what smokers exhale, plus any smoke from the burning end of a cigarette, cigar, or pipe. Secondhand smoke contains more than 4,000 chemicals—and none of them are good for you!

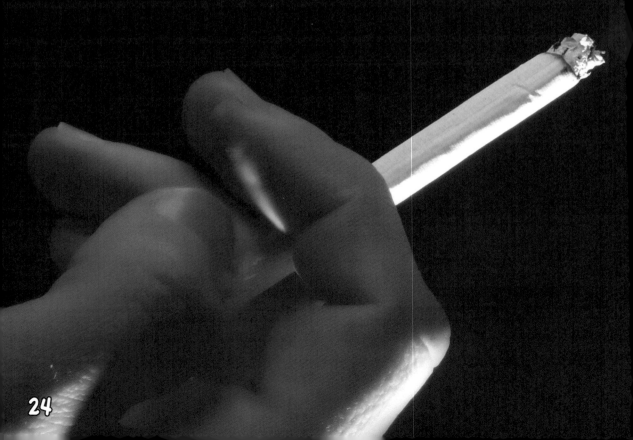

ASK THE DOCTOR

Why are childen more likely to get asthma than adults?

A: Because children's bodies are developing rapidly, anything that gets in the way of their normal growth makes them more vulnerable to injury and illness. Also, children's airways are smaller than adults', so they have more asthma symptoms, like wheezing and shortness of breath, than adults with the same degree of asthma.

Secondhand smoke can both trigger asthma attacks AND make the attacks worse. Preschool children who have never had asthma before are more likely to get it if they breathe secondhand smoke. Scientists believe the smoke *irritates* the air passageways.

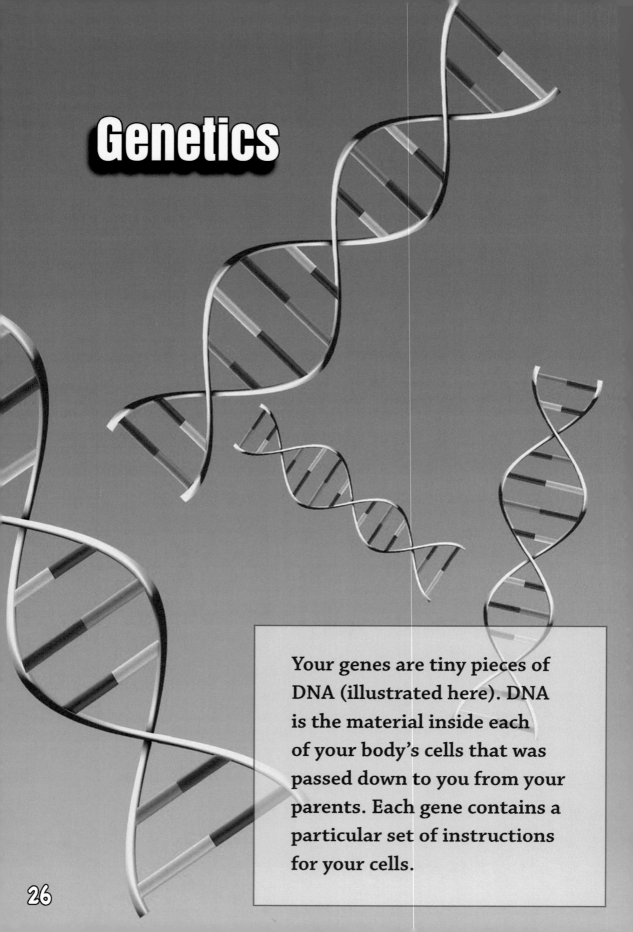

Genetics

Your genes are tiny pieces of DNA (illustrated here). DNA is the material inside each of your body's cells that was passed down to you from your parents. Each gene contains a particular set of instructions for your cells.

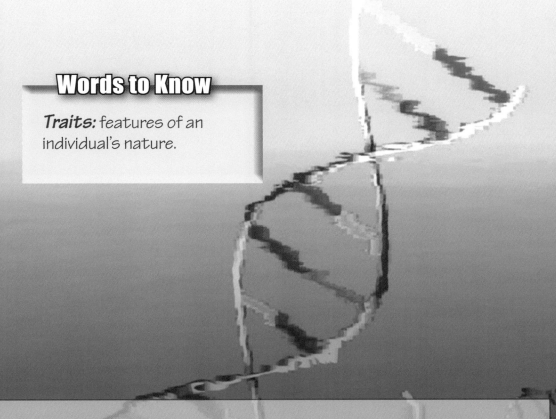

Words to Know

Traits: features of an individual's nature.

Your genes are your body's "blueprint." They are what make you have brown or blonde hair, dark or pale skin, and blue or brown eyes. They also carry the instructions for other *traits*. Some of these traits can make you more likely to get a particular disease or condition.

Scientists believe that about half of all cases of asthma are linked to genetics (while the other half are caused mostly by triggers in the environment). This means if your parents and others in your family have asthma, you're more likely to have it, too.

How Do You Know If You Have Asthma?

If you have periods of wheezing, coughing, and being short of breath, your doctor may start to think you have asthma. You'll need to have some tests to find out for sure.

These tests don't hurt. The doctor will look inside your nose and throat to see if your tissues there are inflamed. He'll listen with a *stethoscope* to your breathing. He may ask you to blow through a device like the one below, a peak flow meter.

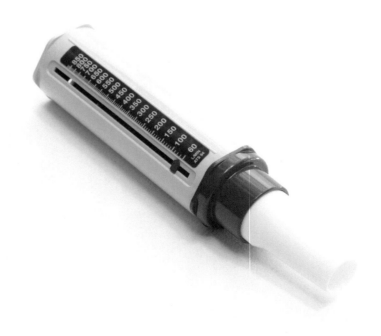

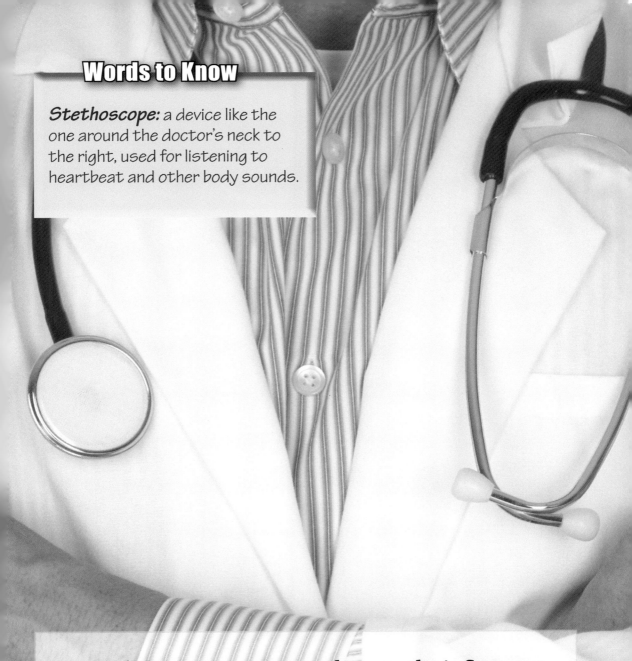

A peak flow meter measures how much air flows out of your lungs when you push it out in one quick blast. Another test uses a machine called a spirometer. For this test, you take deep breaths and push them out as hard as you can into a hose. The spirometer measures how fast and how much you can breathe in and out.

How Is Asthma Treated?

ASK THE DOCTOR

Can you get "high" from using an inhaler?
A: No, you can't. If you use your inhaler too often, the only thing you'll feel is a little dizzy and lightheaded. Your heart may also beat faster. But it won't make you high!

If your doctor decides you have asthma, she will probably want you to take medicine that will help you breathe better.

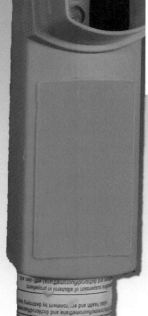

Asthma medicine comes in a few different forms. Some medicines are meant to be inhaled. These often come in packages that look like the gray and white ones on the left page. When you push a button, they release a puff of medicine you suck into your lungs. Other asthma medications are pills you will probably need to take every day. Some medicines act quickly and provide short-term help. Others are long-lasting and are meant to prevent asthma symptoms. Your doctor will help you decide which are best for you.

Inhalers and Nebulizers

An inhaler is shown on this page, and a nebulizer is on the page to the right. Both allow you to breathe in asthma medicine. An inhaler gives a quick puff, while the nebulizer allows you to breathe the medicine steadily.

Did You Know?

Medicines like these are called bronchodilaters, because they dilate (make wider) the bronchial tubes in your lungs. They are also sometimes called "rescue" medications, because they stop an asthma attack that's in progress.

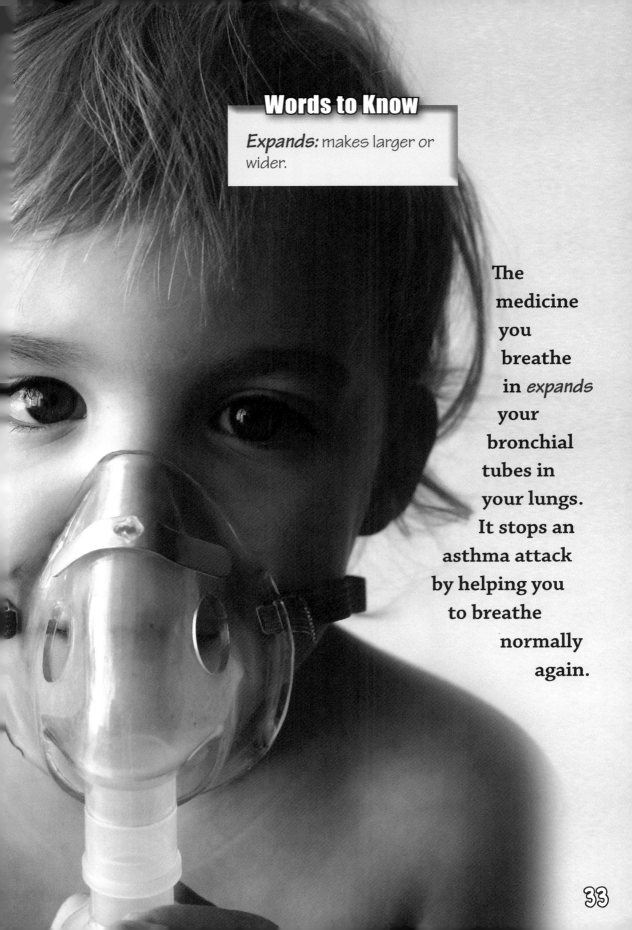

Words to Know

Expands: makes larger or wider.

The medicine you breathe in *expands* your bronchial tubes in your lungs. It stops an asthma attack by helping you to breathe normally again.

33

Steroids

Steroids are a type of chemical that helps *reduce* asthma symptoms by getting rid of some of the swelling and mucus in a person's airways.

Steroids are usually inhaled, often from a package that looks like the one shown on this page. This medicine is good for preventing asthma attacks—but it won't help you when you're in the middle of one.

Words to Know

Reduce: make smaller or make happen less often.

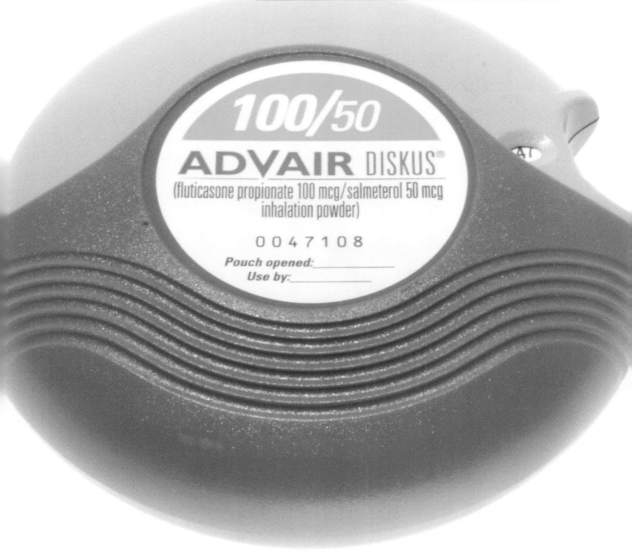

Alternative Treatments

Some people are uncomfortable with taking chemicals to treat their asthma. They may try *alternative* treatments instead, such as yoga (shown here) or acupuncture (shown on the next page.) Doctors agree that both of these can help reduce asthma symptoms.

Yoga exercises make your respiratory system stronger. These exercises improve your lung *function*.

Acupuncture involves placing small needles in certain parts of your body (it doesn't hurt!). It can also help you breathe better.

Words to Know

Alternative: allowing a choice.

Function: ability to do the job something is meant to do.

Both these techniques are based on ancient forms of medicine from Asia. While both can help prevent asthma symptoms, neither is much use when you're actually in the middle of an attack. That's why doctors recommend using these treatments along with medication as needed.

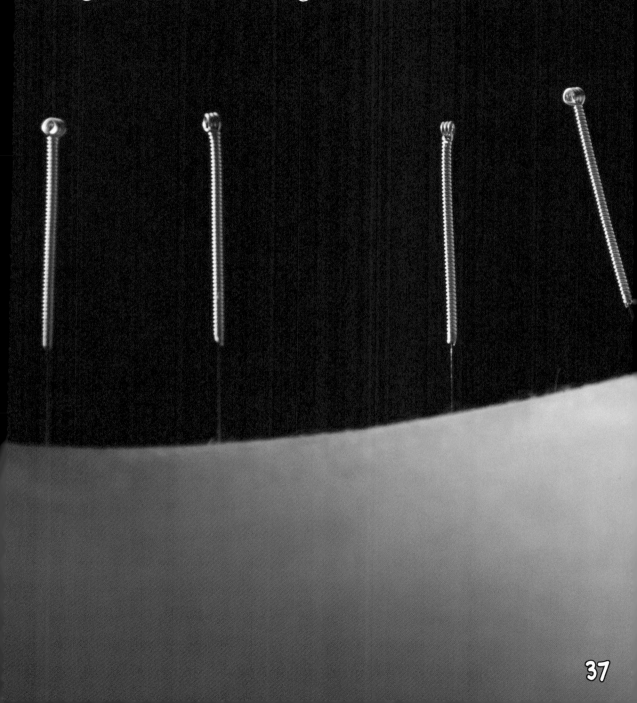

What Happens If You Don't Take Your Medicine?

If you find out you have asthma, it's important to take your medicine. Even if you don't have an asthma attack, you may have ongoing low-level symptoms, such as chest pains, cough, and a stuffy nose. Germs can get stuck in the extra mucus in your airways and make you sick more often with colds.

Taking your medicine helps keep you healthier. It allows you to do all the things you want to without having to gasp for air.

ASK THE DOCTOR

Will I have to take asthma medicine the rest of my life?
A: Maybe—but maybe not. Asthma symptoms often change as you grow, and sometimes you outgrow them alto-gether. Let your doctor know exactly how you're feeling. She may want to adjust your medicine, giving you lower or higher doses as needed. And yes, it's possible you won't always need it. That's a decision for your doctor to make.

38

Will Having Asthma Change Your Life?

Having asthma (or any other illness) means you have to pay more attention to your body. You have to listen to the messages your body gives you. Learning to avoid the triggers that cause you to have asthma (things you're allergic to, for example, or cigarette smoke or emotional stress) can help you control your asthma symptoms better. But that doesn't mean that asthma has to control YOU!

Did You Know?

Your emotions can trigger an asthma attack. When you're upset or stressed, you are much more likely to have asthma symptoms.

41

Can You Still Exercise?

If you have asthma, you may feel like you don't want to exercise. Running around makes you breathe harder, and breathing harder can sometimes trigger asthma. You may also feel like it's hard to get enough oxygen to exercise.

Did You Know?

Try to avoid exercising in air that's very cold, smoky, or polluted.

Many professional athletes have asthma. But they don't let that stop them!

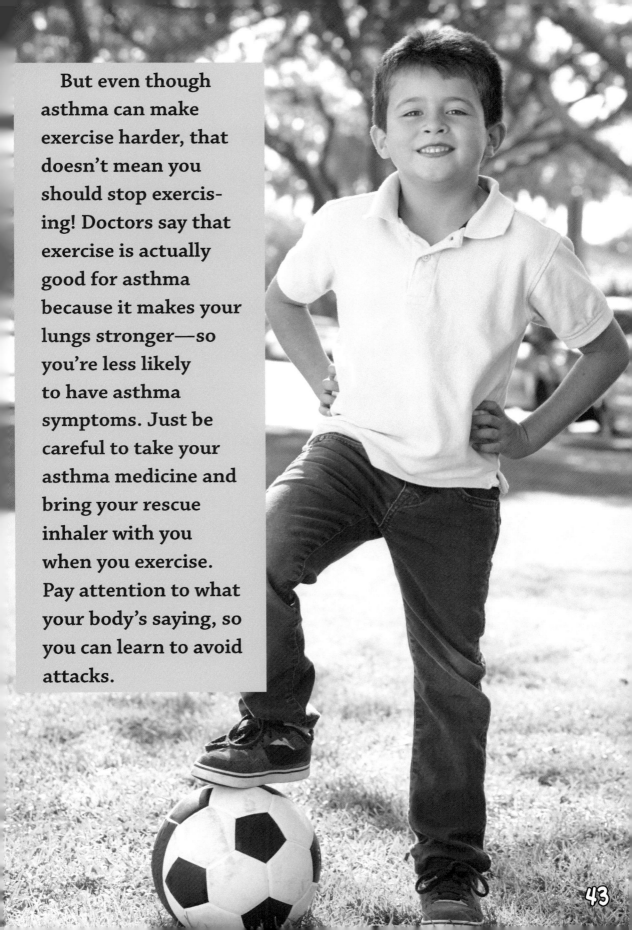

But even though asthma can make exercise harder, that doesn't mean you should stop exercising! Doctors say that exercise is actually good for asthma because it makes your lungs stronger—so you're less likely to have asthma symptoms. Just be careful to take your asthma medicine and bring your rescue inhaler with you when you exercise. Pay attention to what your body's saying, so you can learn to avoid attacks.

Can You Play a Musical Instrument?

Playing a wind instrument like a clarinet, flute, or recorder can be hard if you can't breathe. If you have asthma, you may feel as though you shouldn't bother trying to play one of these instruments.

But remember, you don't need to let asthma control your life! Learning to play a wind instrument can improve your lung function. It can teach you how to breathe more *efficiently*. It can actually help you avoid asthma attacks.

So if you're musical, a wind instrument might be exactly right for you!

Words to Know

Efficiently: in a way that makes the best use of time and effort.

Some doctors are teaching children to play recorders as a way to help them learn how to breathe through an asthma attack. Because asthma attacks are scary, children may breathe faster and make their symptoms worse. Learning to play a recorder helps them learn how to stay calm and focused on their breathing during an asthma attack.

What Is the World Doing About Asthma?

As asthma becomes more and more common, people are working together to find ways to fight this disease. Teaching people more about what asthma is and how it's treated can help kids who may have this condition without even knowing it. Raising money for research will help scientists understand better what causes asthma and how it can be prevented.

Words to Know

Awareness: having knowledge about something.

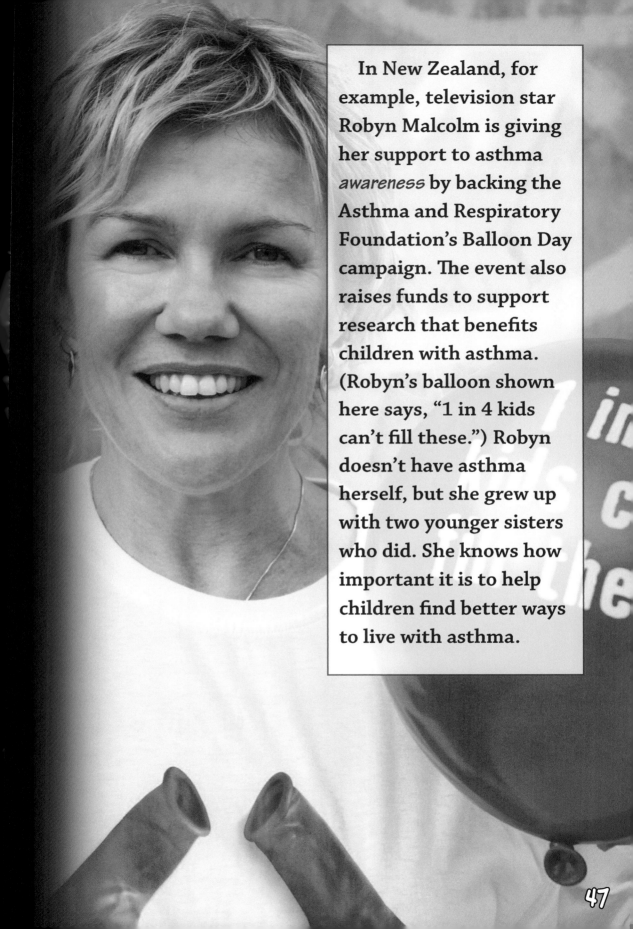

In New Zealand, for example, television star Robyn Malcolm is giving her support to asthma *awareness* by backing the Asthma and Respiratory Foundation's Balloon Day campaign. The event also raises funds to support research that benefits children with asthma. (Robyn's balloon shown here says, "1 in 4 kids can't fill these.") Robyn doesn't have asthma herself, but she grew up with two younger sisters who did. She knows how important it is to help children find better ways to live with asthma.

47

Asthma Research

Scientists are also coming up with new inventions that help them understand and treat asthma more efficiently.

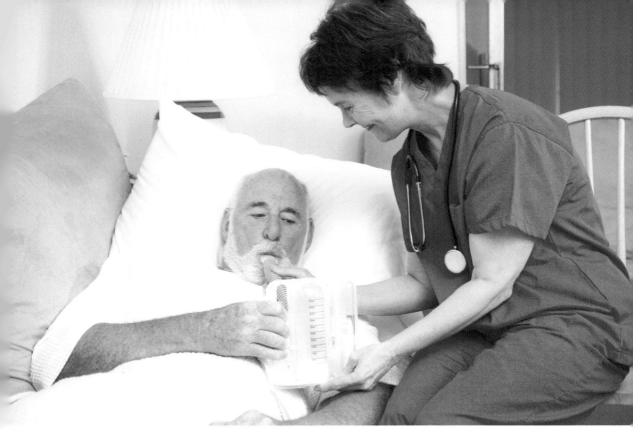

For example, a sensor system that fits in the pocket *monitors* the air around people who have asthma. Researchers can then see what was in the air when a person has an asthma attack. This may help scientists understand better how to prevent attacks.

The asthma monitor shown above helps you monitor your asthma by measuring your lung function. This lets you know if you need to change your behavior or your medication to prevent an asthma attack.

Words to Know

Monitors: keeps a watch on, keeps track of.

Organizations

Because asthma is such a big problem for so many children and adults, people have joined together in *organizations* to fight this condition. Here are just a few of the most important ones:

- World Lung Foundation
- World Allergy Organization
- Global Alliance Against Chronic Respiratory Disease (GARD)
- Asthma UK
- American Lung Association

Words to Know

Organizations: groups of people working together with a plan to achieve a particular goal.

Did You Know?

GARD is a part of the World Health Organization (WHO). It helps individuals and asthma organizations in many countries work together.

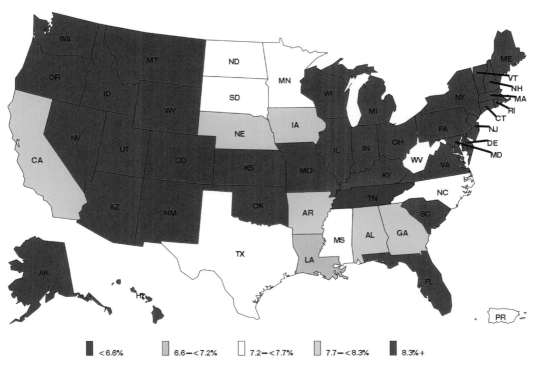

Footnote: Ranges are based on quintiles of the overall prevalence estimates from year 2000 data

Air Pollution and Respiratory Health Branch, National Center for Environmental Health
Centers for Disease Control and Prevention

The map above shows the number of adults who have reported having asthma in each state in 2010. The states colored pink and red are where asthma is most common.

Will I Outgrow Asthma?

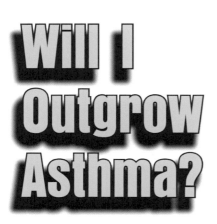

Doctors know that asthma symptoms get better sometimes and even disappear, but they have no way to predict when or if that will happen. They think it depends partly on how old you were when you got asthma and how bad your symptoms were.

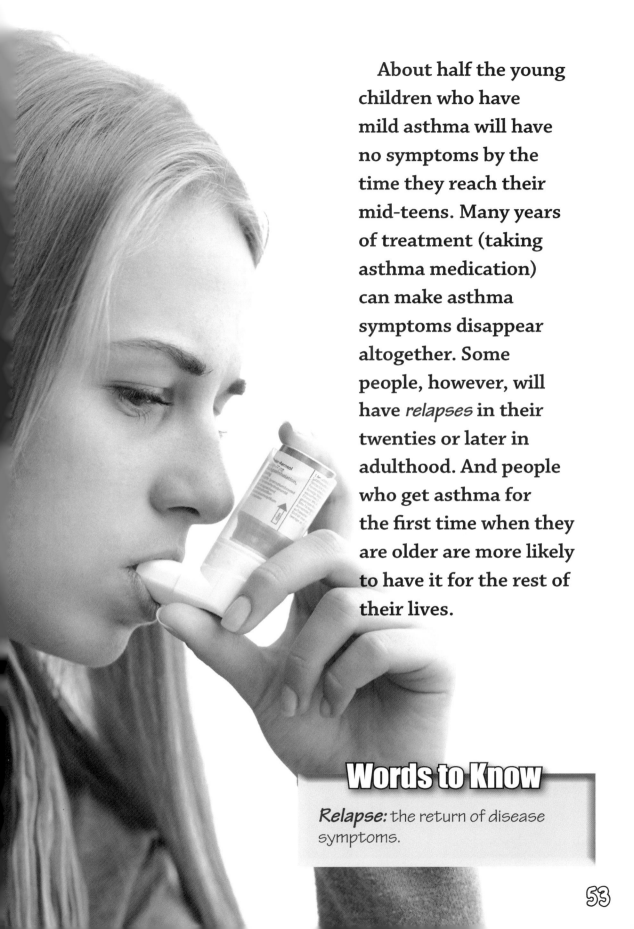

About half the young children who have mild asthma will have no symptoms by the time they reach their mid-teens. Many years of treatment (taking asthma medication) can make asthma symptoms disappear altogether. Some people, however, will have *relapses* in their twenties or later in adulthood. And people who get asthma for the first time when they are older are more likely to have it for the rest of their lives.

Words to Know

Relapse: the return of disease symptoms.

Can Asthma Be Prevented?

Scientists are trying to find ways to stop people from getting asthma. One of the things researchers are looking into is diet.

Studies have shown that teens who don't eat many fruits and vegetables are more likely to have asthma. Other research indicates that the kinds of fruit and vegetables that are brightly colored may contain chemicals and vitamins that help prevent asthma.

Scientists aren't sure yet exactly what the connection is between diet and asthma—but it never hurts to eat more fruits and vegetables!

Real Kids

Leon has had asthma since he was five months old. Thanks to the medication he still uses and always carries with him, his asthma is now under control.

Leon loves ballroom dancing. He's won nine gold medals and was first in all the categories in which he participated. He also plays rugby and is looking forward to going to his first Boy Scout camp soon. He's not letting asthma get in the way of his life.

Another Real Kid

When you look at Katie, you don't see a "sick" child. When you hear about her great ability to play hockey or soccer, you don't hear about the medications she has to take several times a day so she can play. When you know about her good marks in school, you don't know about the war going on inside her body.

Katie has asthma. She has to battle for what most children take for granted—to be able to breathe. There are times when each breath is a struggle and being afraid is normal.

Katie is doing her part—taking her medications (even when she sometimes wishes she didn't have to), avoiding her asthma triggers (like not being able have a cat), and being an amazing athlete (even though there are times when her chest hurts a lot). Does it all make a difference? When we asked Katie this question, her answer included this example: "Some winters I miss at least fourteen days of school. This year, I've missed only three so far." For Katie, it's all about being able to be a regular, active kid who loves to play sports.

(The Lung Association, an organization working to fight asthma, tells about Katie on its website, www.lung.ca/diseases-maladies/asthma-asthme/faces-visages/katie_e.php)

Find Out More

These websites will tell you more about asthma:

Asthma: American Lung Association
www.lung.org/lung-disease/asthma

The Asthma Society of Canada
www.asthma.ca

Asthma UK
www.asthma.org.uk

CDC Asthma
www.cdc.gov/asthma

GINA: Global Initiative for Asthma
www.ginasthma.org

MedlinePlus: Asthma
www.nlm.nih.gov/medlineplus/asthma.html

What Is Asthma?
www.nhlbi.nih.gov/health/health-topics/topics/asthma

World Health Organization: Asthma
www.who.int/topics/asthma/en

Index

Picture Credits

Dreamstime.com:

8: Alexander Shalamov

11: Darrenw

12: Sebastian Kaulitzki

14: Hongqi Zhang (aka Michael Zhang)

15: Eduard Härkönen

16: Imagepointphoto

17: Jirsa

18: Sebastian Kaulitzki

19: Alila07

20: Stuart Miles

21: Rob3000

22-23: Ramunas Bruzas

24-25: Henrischmit

26-27: Rolffimages

28: Tawesit

29: Katrina Brown

30: Robert Elias

31: Jirsa

32: Peter Elvidge

33: Baronoskie

35: Robert Sholl

36: Shotsstudio

37: Yanik Chauvin

39: Candybox Images

41: Tammy Mcallister

42: Nagy-bagoly Ilona

43: Monkey Business Images

45: Elena Milevska

48: Jonathan Ross

49: Lisa F. Young

52-53: Alexander Raths

54: Maffboy

55: Dave Bredeson

57: Catalin Petolea

58-59: Dawn Hudson

13: Environmental Protection Agency | EPA.gov

47: The Asthma Foundation | asthmafoundation.org.nz

51: Centers for Disease Control | www.cdc.gov

To the best knowledge of the publisher, all other images are in the public domain. If any image has been inadvertently uncredited, please notify Village Earth Press, Vestal, New York 13850, so that rectification can be made for future printings.

About the Author

Rae Simons has written many books for young adults and children.

About the Consultant

Elise DeVore Berlan, MD, MPH, FAAP, is a faculty member of the Division of Adolescent Health at Nationwide Children's Hospital and an Assistant Professor of Clinical Pediatrics at the Ohio State University College of Medicine. She completed her fellowship in adolescent medicine at Children's Hospital Boston and obtained a master's degree in public health at the Harvard School of Public Health. Dr. Berlan completed her residency in pediatrics at the Children's Hospital of Philadelphia, where she also served an additional year as chief resident. She received her medical degree from the University of Iowa College of Medicine.